Blooming Within!

BANDANA ROY

BookLeaf Publishing

India | USA | UK

Presentation by *BookLeaf Publishing*

Web: www.bookleafpub.com

E-mail: info@bookleafpub.com

ISBN: 9789363313453

First edition 2024

To selfless womanhood.

CONTENTS

Chapter 1

I will always be there for you (Motherhood).

Chapter 2

Do the little you every day: (Motivational).

11) Beauty.
12) Breath.
13) Embrace positivity.
14) IKIGAI.
15) Stages of life.
16) Pause.
17) Fly.
18) Do the little you every day.
19) The beauty of now.

Chapter 3

Broken but Beautiful: (Womanhood).

Chapter 4

Silent Truth: (To the Society).

Chapter 5

Gratitude: (to the almighty)

Chapter 1

I will always be there for
you. —Motherhood.

I will always be there for you!

Like a steadfast old tree,
Holding tight to the roots of your life,
Caring, loving, and watching over you,
Always thinking of your happiness,
       I will always be there for you.

From your first tiny steps,
Through all the years you have grown,
From being close to me
To fly on your own,
Searching for your dreams—
       I will always be there for you.

Yes, keep going forward,
Don't look back if you don't need to,
But if there is a day you struggle,
And life feels too hard to bear,
Come back to me without worry,
            I will always be there for you.

Like your own shadow,
I ask for nothing in return.
I will keep you in my prayers,
Only to see you safe and sound.
I will always be there for you.

She is Me!

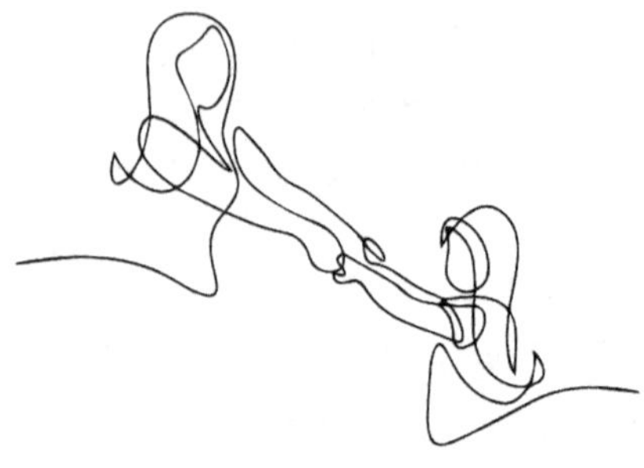

The deeply instilled feeling within me,
I am raising my daughter as my mother raised
me.
I once vowed never to give my life away,
But the moment I became a mom,
　　　All my identities quietly stepped aside.

I look back now and see,
Without knowing, I have become like her,
It flows through me naturally,
To always stand at the back of the line,
　Prioritising everyone else's needs above mine.

But for my daughter, I dream a different way—
I wish for her to thrive, to rise,
To seek her dreams without compromise,
　　To place herself first, with no fear, no delay.

Yet how?
Won't she mirror me as I mirrored my mother?
Centuries of truth, so deeply wired.
But life has shown me:
If I wish her not to be me,
I must break free,
Visualise and live the woman.
I want her to be.

Nature and Mother!

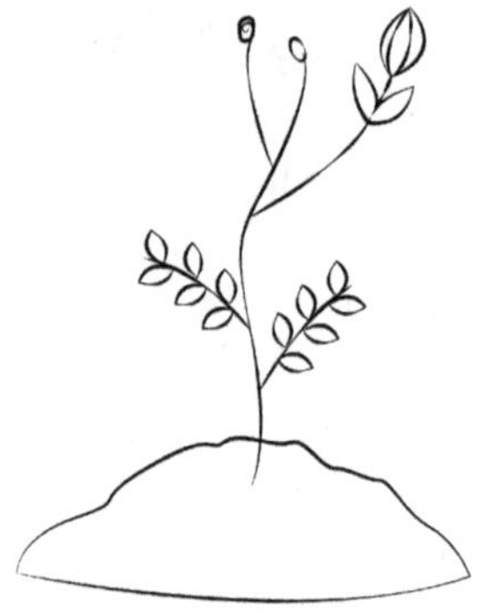

When a sprout breaks through the soil,
A new life takes form.
The soil splits in gentle pain,
      Yet there is joy in this strain.

Seeing the tender leaves emerge,
A glimpse of fresh life.
For a mother, this one moment,
    Outweighs all her treasures and strife.

She bears any pain without a word,
But shields her child with all her might.
The bond between mother and child—
      Pure and boundless as light.

With the power of Mother Nature,
Each creature finds its way.
She is the core of all we are,
Every mother is a whole world in herself.

When you first called me 'Mom'!

A string of happiness flooded my veins,
It brought me a sense of joy in living,
Small tears in the corners of my eyes,
The feeling of being complete as a woman.

When you first called me 'Mom'!

I felt a great sense of purpose,
Now, my life revolves around this word,
I play all the other roles to live,
But this one word defines my identity.

When you first called me 'Mom'!

A melodious song reached my heart,
Filled music in my body and soul,
I felt the reason for my being,
These three letters became my world.

Motherhood!

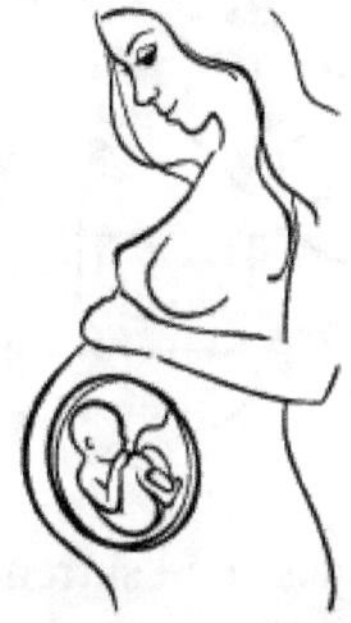

I create, protect, nurture and care,
I feel heartbreak when I see you fall,
I rejoice, seeing you rise,
I care for you more than myself.

You are meant to be a separate self,
But I will care for you till my last breath,
The moment you were born, I ceased to be me,
I am a mother first; everything else comes next.

I don't care if it's right or wrong,
To give you all that I have.
But you must strive for your dreams,
You will always have my blessings.

It's not a choice, but it comes naturally,
To choose you over everything else,
I wish to give you that protection,
Forever, until my last breath.

You are home, Mom!

Pillars of selflessness and surrender,
Weaving the lives of all of us,
You make this house of brick and mortar,
What we call a home.

You decorate it with pearls of affection,
You colour its walls with love,
With every prayer of yours,
You make this home a divine temple.

The morning starts with your smile,
The night ends with your lullaby,
Every corner of our home,
It brightened with your aura, Mom.

The roof of this home is made of your patience,
Your hopes are the rays of light,
You always bring all of us together,
You are next to God for us, Mom.

Just You (A Mother's Wish)

Parenting is a lesson we learn each day,
It is a journey of love in its unique way.
Through trials and errors, both big and small,
   Every fall, every rise—I have faced them all.

Whenever these memories come through,
Smile at the love that carried us, too.
I bless you for reaching for the stars so high,
   Your triumphs will always light up my sky.

Fly with courage, chase every dream,
Life is a river, ever-changing its stream.
But whenever you witness "motherly love."
   Recall the moments and bonding we have.

I am no one special, just a heart that beats,
But you are my legacy, my soul's retreat.
Emotions are priceless, can't be bought or sold,
    In this world of gains and losses, it is untold.

I ask for nothing, no grand display,
Just call me "Mom" in your own sweet way.
I raised you with all that I thought was right,
    And you, my child, gave my life its light.

Mornings start with your laughter's song,
Evenings feel short, though the days are long.
When my time comes to bid goodbye,
    Hold me close, with love in your eyes.

Foundation

I will never forget it, Mom,
The quiet strength of your love.
You made our joy your life's purpose,
    Burying your dreams without hesitation.

Every choice you made whispered sacrifice,
Yet you asked for nothing, only gave.
You shaped our lives with unspoken courage,
Fighting battles we never saw,
       Carrying burdens we never felt.

Each meal you prepared held silent care,
Your desires set aside, unnoticed, unspoken.
In a world where love often seeks a return,
    Yours remained pure, selfless, eternal.

You are the foundation of all I believe,
The quiet hero who built my world.
Your love is my guide, my strength, my faith—
The unshakable base of everything I am.

Innocence!

Your laughter fills my world with boundless joy,
Your smile, so pure, is my brightest light.
When you cry, my heart aches,
      But your smile brings sunshine back.

Each tiny step you take is my greatest pride,
Your little hands reach for the stars,
As if you hold the magic of the universe.
Your wonder at birds, trees, and skies
        Reminds me of endless dreams.

Your soft words, unclear yet sweet,
Are melodies I treasure deeply.
When you call me "Mom,"
My world feels complete.
Through you, I relive the magic of childhood,
Each moment with you, my dearest,
Is a joy beyond measure.

Lullaby!

From the corners of your sleepy eyes,
Softly, gently, the dream fairy flies.
She whispers low and hums her tune,
    To take you where the magic blooms.

The dream fairy arrives with gentle grace,
To lead you to her magical place.
A castle shines with silver light,
A golden bed glows through the night.
A mattress of flowers, soft and sweet,
    In a mother's love, your dreams will meet.

The dream fairy arrives with gentle grace,
To lead you to her magical place.
Close your eyes as the calm winds play,
        Rocking your cradle far away.

In her arms, you will gently lie,
With every swing, time quickly flies.
The dream fairy arrives with gentle grace,
  To lead you to her magical place.

The moon smiles down from the sky above,
While stars sing songs of pure love.
Fireflies dance with their endless glow,
Lighting your path wherever you go.
The dream fairy arrives with gentle grace,
To lead you to her magical place.

Chapter 2

Do the little you, each day. -
Motivational

Beauty!

As the years fly by, the glow of youth may fade,
But the light of the mind grows stronger,
unshaken, unfazed.
True beauty is not found in the mirror;
It resides in the thoughts we nurture,
In the wisdom we possess,
      And the kindness we show.

Looks will fade as time takes them,
But the way we touch lives,
The love we give freely,
Will remain long after.
Beauty is not what the eyes perceive,
It is what the heart feels,
And the legacy we leave
In the minds and hearts of others.

Breathe!

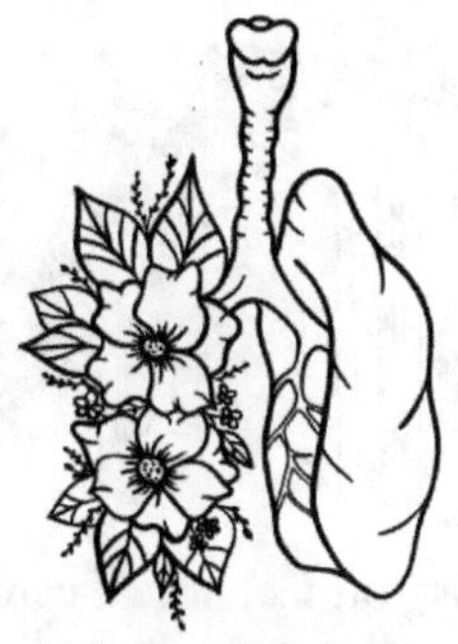

Recognise when it is time to slow down,
Take a break; let the tension drown.
Just breathe, in and out, so deep,
Close your eyes, and find your peace.

Feed your mind with ideas anew,
Read books, and let knowledge brew.
Broaden your vision, expand your sight,
Give yourself the gift of light.

For life is not just hustle and haste,
It lives in the breaths that we embrace.
In this very moment, find your grace,
Breathe deep; slow your pace.

Even when the world feels heavy,
When the path ahead seems unsteady,
Take a break, pause the fight,
Just breathe, let in the light.

Embrace Positivity!

When life deals you its hardest cards,
There lies a lesson, though it seems hard.
When fairness fades and nothing seems right,
The strength within you will resume the fight.

When solitude wraps you in its embrace,
You are reaching nearer to your own sacred
space.
When challenges arise, and joy seems rare,
Believe that your path is leading you
somewhere.

Remember, when life strikes with its heaviest
blow,
Its truths are revealed, and your wisdom unfolds.
With every strong hammer that life throws,
You are being shaped into a diamond that glows.

Stay positive.

IKIGAI!

You are unique, believe it true,
One special gift that differentiates you.

The world won't bend to fit your plan,
But that one thing brings joy that spans.

When others doubt and consider you small,
That one thing keeps you standing tall.

Whenever you feel low in confidence,
That one thing reminds you of your strength.

Love, nourish, struggle, and refine,
That one thing makes your spirit shine.

For it is the heart of who you are,
That one thing makes you a star.

Stages of Life

Life flows like a gentle stream,
It seems to be changing each year.
As toddlers, we learn to walk and play,
Exploring the world in our small way.
In childhood, we grow and learn,
Laying the base with innocence and fun.
Teenage brings lessons, hard but true,
Each mistake shapes a better you.
Youth is for dreams and building your name,
Starting small but chasing big fame.
Midlife is where you truly see,
The person you have grown and meant to be.
Old age whispers, "Cherish it all,
Each moment's precious, be itbig or small."
The secret to life is simple yet true:
Stay happy at every stage; it's all up to you.

Pause!

In the next challenging moment,
A tiny tear appears in the corner of your eye.
Pause, and remember the blessings you hold—
You can choose to weep or to feel alright.
Mistakes will happen,
Let them drift away with kindness.
Criticism may seem the easier road,
But it hurts you more than it affects others.
Build yourself up,
Become the one whose inner peace matters
most.
Outwardly, you may react as you have practised,
But let your soul should remain divine.
If you find joy in simply being with yourself,
That is the truest love—
For you,
And for all.

Fly!

When your thoughts and dreams align,
You are poised to fly, to touch the sky.

When all seems okay, yet solitude feels divine,
You are poised to fly, to soar so high.

When you resist life's imposed norms,
You are poised to fly, to rise beyond.

When doubts no longer cast their shadows,
You are poised to fly, to rise from the shallows.

Awake or dreaming, when eyes see life the
same,
You are poised to fly, to live your name.

Fueled with confidence, eager for the new,
Embrace the challenges, and fly.

Do the Little You Every Day!

Write a few lines, just a small piece,
Or decorate a corner with gentle ease.
Call a loved one, share your heart,
Or make a snack, your little art.
Be proud of what your hands create,
Smile at each passion you celebrate.
Your art is a place to safely land,
A mirror of life, both small and grand.
Life is too short to chase perfection,
Embrace the flaws; they are your reflection.
In each creation, feel the glow,
Of love for what you choose to show.
Treat each day as a cherished gift,
Let your spirit rise and freely lift.
And when the day is finally through,
Give a smile and pat the better you.

The beauty of now!

The greatest skill, a precious vow;
To learn the art of being happy now.
The past, a shadow, holds pain we replay,
The future is shaped depends by what we do
today.
Care for yourself; tend to your needs,
And watch as it blooms in life's seeds.
It matters not if we are young or old,
Small acts of progress bring peace to our core.
So don't hold back; embrace what's near,
Find joy in the moment; let clarity steer.
The rest will follow, it's never too late,
Live in the now, and rewrite your fate.

Chapter 3.
Broken but Beautiful - Womanhood

Love and Freedom!

There is a fine line so thin, unseen,
Between love's embrace and no feeling.
In love, emotions take the heart on a daring ride,
  Beyond comfort, beyond money, they survive.

From your eyes, a bitter sting,
A silent push, a broken wing.
In those glances, warmth so true,
     I found a world where dreams grew.

Yet, in that flight, I found my skies,
Freedom whispered through teary eyes.
Love once bound now sets me free,
     To soar, to dream, to simply be.

Throughout this life's journey,
Emotions weave a tale so bold.
In love, we find both joy and pain,
In freedom, we rise, and we live again.

Loner!

Surrounded by many, yet I stand alone,
Smiles all around, but I feel unknown.
The pressure to fit, to blend, to be,
In forced smiles, I lose sight of me.
Is this what society calls connection?
Perhaps, but it's not my reflection.
Though it stings, I won't pretend,
In this solitude, I find my friend.
The best version of me grows in stillness,
In moments of quiet, away from the noise.
Whether lost in a book or letting my thoughts
flow,
I find peace in these simple moments alone.
In solitude, I discover what's true,
The beauty of life lies in being you.

Self-love

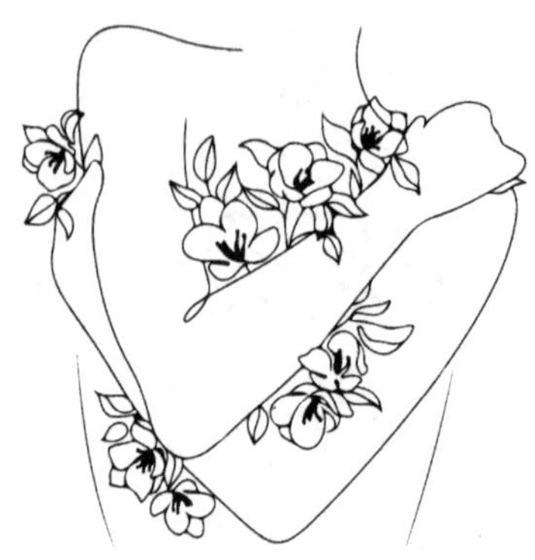

It took me decades
To reach this place,
I hold the remote—my life, my pace.
I see it now,
The love I seek from you,
Begins with loving myself first.
For my glorious life story,
And to make my dreams come true,
It's first a vision in my head, then clear in view.
The mantra is simple,
Show up each day—
And love yourself along the way.

Respect!

Cherish the hearts that go the extra mile,
For they are the ones who restore your smile.
Embrace those who brighten your darkest days,
A simple "thank you" can go such a long way.
To those who work to uplift and inspire,
Show them respect; it's all they require.
Don't overlook the ones who stand by your side,
Their presence, a treasure, should never be
denied.
The bonds we nurture, the ties we keep,
They are shaped by words, kind and deep.
A gentle apology, a heartfelt embrace,
Can mend what's broken and fill the space.
Respect is a gift, both priceless and true,
The more you give, the more it comes back to
you.

My way!

My dreams,
a coffee,
a little progress every day.

My ups,
My downs,
My shades of just grey.

My laugh,
My cry,
A child in me who wants to play.

My pen,
My writing,
My music on replay.

My choice,
My life,
I wish to live my way.

Grace!

The world whispers a tale too sweet,
Of princes on steeds, of lives complete.
But fairytales fade, and truth reveals,
    No knight will save you; no dream is sealed.

In reality, love comes with weight,
Expectations, conditions, and fate.
No saviour waits with outstretched hands,
        Only you can conquer life's demands.

Life isn't perfect; it bends and breaks,
Built on courage, risks, and stakes.
Ride your path through storm and sky,
        Feel the earth, let your spirit fly.

You need no arms to shield your way,
Your strength will guide you every day.
In your scars lies beauty untold,
        In your hands, the power to mould.

Be your grace, your guiding light,
No borrowed dreams, no borrowed might.
For in this world, what truly thrives,
Is the woman who builds her own life.

To My Younger Self

Dear younger me,
Here's a truth to set you free:
Don't try to please everyone you meet,
     It's a game you'll never beat.

Find peace within your heart's song,
Life is yours to paint all along.
You can't control the world's pace,
   But face each challenge with steady grace.

Make knowledge your most precious aim,
With learning and growth, you'll win the game.
Your experiences are treasures to hold,
   Work hard, and a beautiful life will unfold.

It's okay to put yourself first,
Follow your dreams, quench your thirst.
Don't lose yourself in others' demands,
      Hold on tight to your own plans.

The world may push, may pull, may plead,
But guard your heart—that's all you need.
Walk your path, let your soul explore,
And watch your spirit forever soar.

Time Teaches You!

With time, I have come to understand,
Life moves forward, even without those we once
held in hand.
I have seen how love is torn apart,
Leaves scars etched deep within the heart.
Even the happiest moments don a bittersweet
hue,
Their warmth fades, yet their absence feels true.
Time flows on, and I often find,
A dreamer at heart, still lost in my mind.
But time gently whispers, "Let go, forgive,
Life is short—learn to truly live."
So, I give thanks to those who cared,
Who believed in me and the journey we shared.

Reflection!

Growing up, I remember well,
The fears, the doubts, a living hell.
A powerless feeling so hard to shake,
    Following others, no path to make.

Life was filled with self-pity's chain,
Dreams of tomorrow easing the pain.
Promises were made, yet goals would stray,
    Years and decades slipped away.

Until one day, I looked inside,
Reading, reflecting, no place to hide.
The world stayed still, but I could see,
    The power to change was always in me.

Ignorance had fed my strife,
But learning brought light to my life.
I wish I'd known when I was small,
    The strength within can conquer all.

Now I know, and I'll share this truth,
A life of smiles is the greatest proof.
To learn, to grow, and help others rise,
This will be my journey—my biggest prize.

My Dream House

No matter how small my nest will be,
A place that's wholly, finally, me.
The undone bed in the candle's glow,
    Abstract paintings in colours that flow.

Every corner, a piece of my soul,
Not bound to anyone else's control.
In my dream house, I will be just me,
No need for approval; it is finally free.

Just my poems, a quiet crowd,
A cosy bed where dreams are allowed.
A corner for books to call my own,
    A place to weave my words alone.

I will decorate my world with my words,
My dreams of decades, my experiences unheard.
No more masks, no roles to play,
Just me, at last, in my way.

Chapter 4

Silent Truth - To the Society.

Mask!

I cannot live as I truly am;
To survive, I wear a mask.
My mask takes on many faces—
For society, it is a smile,
For relatives, a mask of care,
       For myself, to simply fit in.

I stay far from my truths,
Running fast, so fast,
Even my shadow can't catch me.
Yet, in this hurried escape,
Thoughts creep into my mind,
       But the mask quickly silences them.

When the will to live wanes,
Existence feels hollow,
And life's weight presses down.
In the crowd, I only see masks,
Concealing each person's truths—
          A grand, endless play.

Then comes the piercing thought:
Am I, too, just a character in this act?
I search for purpose and find none,
Only a desperate need to be alone.
For whatever my truth may be,
It is the only real part of me.

A question!

They tell us, "Give your best,
Rise, shine, move ahead."
But no one speaks of those who pause,
Who give their all and forget themselves.
Women build homes, not just walls,
   Layered with love, stitched with sacrifice.

Day by day, they weave a life.
For others, sidelining their desires.
Morning to night, hands never still,
Cooking, cleaning, caring—
         Hearts full, yet empty.

Their laughter fades,
Drowned by the hum of chores.
Years slip by,
Like sand through fingers.

Dreams buried under piles of laundry,
Hopes lost in the silence of waiting.
One day, they look in the mirror,
        Searching for the girl they once knew.

She is there, somewhere,
Hidden beneath wrinkles and weariness.
But now, the home feels heavier,
Its walls are too close, too quiet.
A home built with love,
        But lined with forgotten desires.

And they wonder:
Is this all?
Is this what life was meant to be?
Their hearts ache, not for others,
but for themselves—
For the life they gave away,
Without even realising it.

Rising Again

When women step back into the world of work,
They carry not just resumes but stories—
Years spent nurturing, building, giving,
Yet all the world sees are the "gaps."
A pause, they call it, as if she stood still,
    But in those years, she became a force.

Balancing sleepless nights and endless days,
She mastered patience, resilience, and grace.
Her skills may not fit into neat columns,
But her strength is carved into her soul.
She knows the weight of responsibility,
    And the art of holding worlds together.

Each rejection stings like a sharp reminder,
That society values the clock over character.
But does a spreadsheet show the wisdom
Of calming storms or leading with love?

Their worth can not be measured by years
worked,
But by the strength forged in sacrifice.
And when they rise again,
The world will stand witness to their light.

Shaken Stage

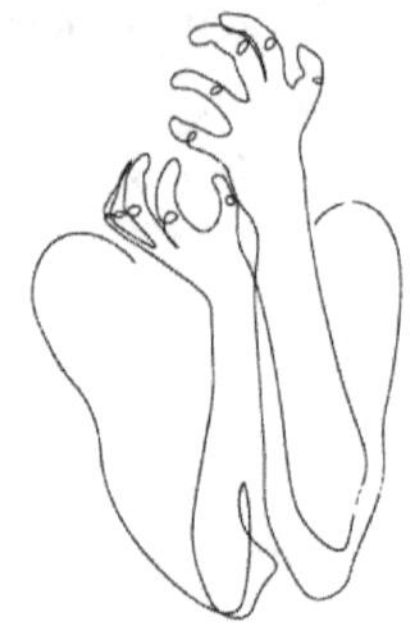

She carried the weight of their world,
Giving her all to build a home.
Dreams and youth set aside,
      But his words still cut her deep.

What she thought was love,
Turned into blame and silence.
Her sacrifices unseen,
Her worth questioned,
      Until her dreams faded into ash.

For the sake of the little ones,
She held on, piecing together the cracks.
But a truth slowly rose—
      Her value wasn't his to decide.

Through tears, she found her strength,
Not in his eyes but within herself.
And though the stage was shaken,
She stood firm,
Rebuilding a life where she mattered.

The Guilt of being a girl

I look back and wonder why,
Why did this guilt follow me?
It is there, though I can not say how,
A weight I have carried, even now.
They said, "Be good, stay in line,
Be sweet, be quiet, don't cross the signs."
Each time I choose to walk my way,
The guilt returns as if to stay.
I have spent my life trying to please,
Fitting in, keeping the peace.
Dreaming of love for who I am,
But I was holding back, afraid to stand.
I long for someone who truly sees,
Not just my gender or face but me.
To know my heart and truly understand
The strength I hold and the dreams I have.

The Journey of One Night

The night she was married,
She crossed a threshold of no return,
Leaving behind the warmth of her world,
    To step into another, unfamiliar and new.

From cherished daughter to dutiful
daughter-in-law,
From being loved to learning to serve.
Her laughter, once free and loud,
    Now softened, tucked away in silence.

In one fleeting night,
Her world turned upside down.
The girl she was fades into memory,
As she tries to embrace this unknown journey.
A thousand emotions swirl within her—
    Fear, hope, loss, resilience.

With each step, she learns to balance,
To hold herself steady amidst the change.
It's a story of courage,
Of leaving, of becoming,
Of finding herself again,
In a world she's just begun to call her own.

Rise like the dawn!

Since my birth, I have always seen,
Women are sidelined, unheard and unseen.
To me, it feels so natural to suppress my dreams,
 To chase others' joy, even if it means losing me.

Growing up meant seeking approvals,
As a girl, survival was tougher than usual.
But slowly, I became the woman I feared,
The one I resented as a teenager.
They speak of self-love, but I am the flame,
Burning for others, forgetting my name.
They say, "Put yourself first before you melt,"
 Yet I was born selfless — that's all I have ever
                        felt.

But maybe, just maybe, the truth is here:
To love myself doesn't mean to disappear.
I can tend to my flame and still give light —
I will rise like the dawn, not fade in the night.

What I Wanted as a Teen!

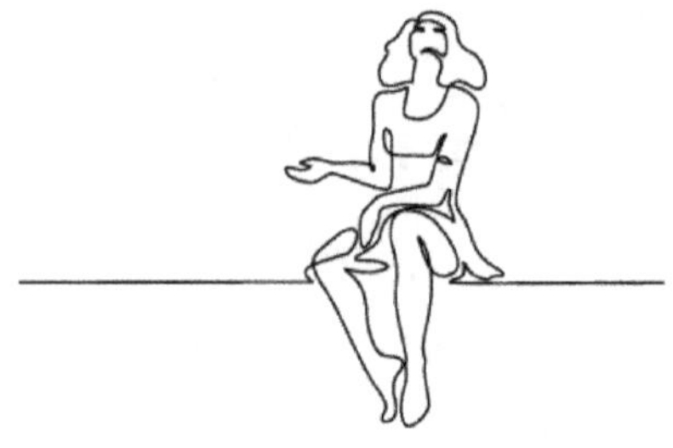

I wished to close my eyes for a while,
    And forget the rules that steal my smile.

I wanted to live, even just for a day,
    Without worrying about my safety.

I just wanted to hold your hand,
    Without thinking of your belongings.

I wanted to laugh at the silliest joke,
    Without worrying about what others think.

I dreamt of flying like birds in the sky,
    Not held back by the thought, I can't try.

All I asked was one chance of truth,
Let me try before calling me through.

Temper!

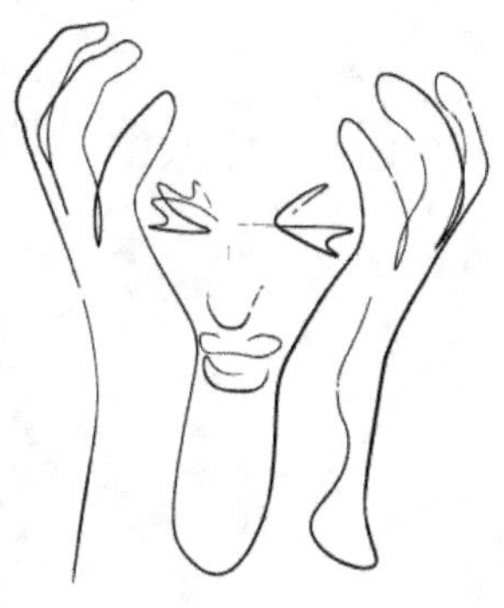

Growing up, I often faced,
A temper threw a harsh disgrace.
No fault of mine, yet there it stayed,
The fault was theirs, in anger displayed.
A lack of control, no patience to find,
No calm, no peace, no thoughtful mind.
The moment may feel too wild to bear
But the choice is ours; it's always there.
You can frown and make it worse,
Or break the cycle, end the curse.
Anger harms health and the bonds we keep,
It sows self-doubt and pain that's deep.
The words you say, the harm they do,
They echo back and hurt you, too.
For in your heart, the truth you know,
Temper hampers the chance to grow.

Chapter 5

Gratitude

Growth

Life is not a competition,
But a path meant to be walked with purpose.
Each moment offers a chance to learn,
Each step, an opportunity to become.

The only comparison worth making
Is with the person you were yesterday.
Growth is not in racing ahead,
But in moving closer to your truest self.

Happiness isn't found in applause or approval,
It lives quietly in the choices you make,
In the love you show yourself,
And the strength you find in the struggles.
Every effort, no matter how small,
Shapes the story you are writing.

This life is yours to create,
A masterpiece only you can paint.

Gratitude

When life feels lacking,
Step beyond your walls.
See the poor carrying hunger and hope-
Your meal becomes a blessing.
Notice those waiting for hours to move
forward—
Your car feels like a gift.
Watch the vendors tirelessly working—
Your job seems easier.
Observe the delivery boy braving the elements-
Your comforts grow precious.
Gratitude blooms when you shift your gaze,
Not to what's missing,
But to what others endure,
And to what you already hold.

My Writing

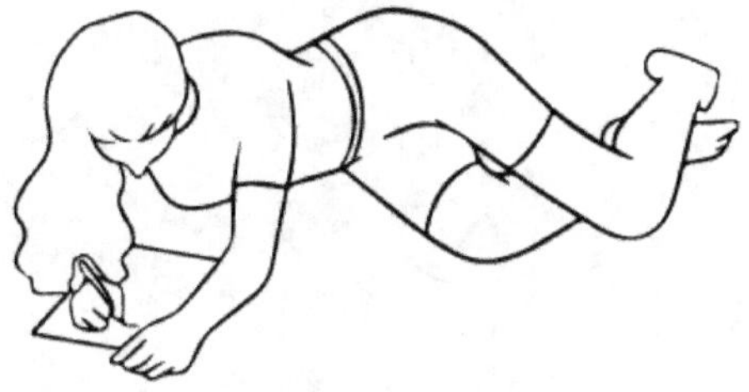

Life may not look like the dreams I once had,
But in writing, I find my refuge, my pride.
Words hold my emotions, shaping my world,
A quiet joy that makes me whole.
I recall moments on stage, the fire within,
The applause, the cheers—proof of my purpose.
Praise for my book feels like an embrace,
A fulfilment can replace.
In writing, I find both strength and peace,
A life complete, a heart at ease.

Sleep Like a Baby

The greatest blessing, the sweetest peace,
It is a heart at rest, a mind at ease.
To work with purpose throughout the day,
    Then drift to sleep in a carefree way.

Have you felt the joy, the quiet thrill,
Of using your time to climb upstairs?
When, inch by inch, your goals come near,
    And dreams feel vivid, alive, and clear.

Life is a puzzle, piece by piece,
One step forward brings steady ease.
When you care for the moment, the present hour,
    You unlock life's gentle, guiding power.

So I treasure each day; it is a grace,
And go to bed with a smile on my face.
For there is no joy that compares to this,
Sleeping like a baby, wrapped in bliss.

Waves of sea

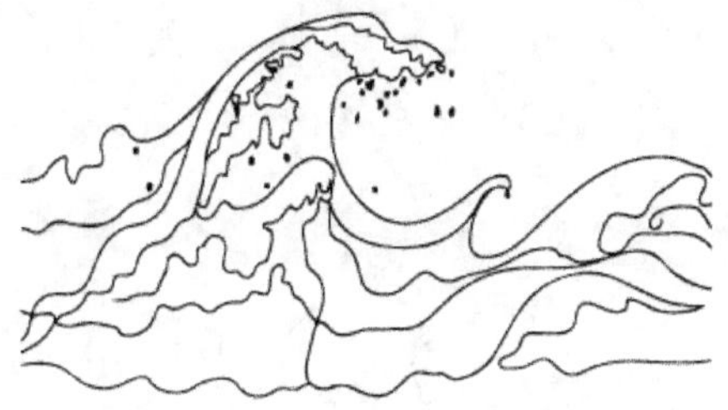

The waves of the sea,
dancing, floating, wild and free.

Coming with a roar,
slowing down towards the shore.

Rhyming with the wind,
together, till the end.

Gently washing over your feet,
it's their own pleasant way to greet.

They travel from far away,
Teaching you not to stop on the way.

Morning

The first touch of the rising sun,
awakening of quiet earth.

A drop of dews on tender leaves,
Freshness flows with every breath.

Flowers opening the petals,
with a pleasant, cold wind.

Singing birds on the tree,
dancing, jumping, flying free.

Depth and pleasure all around,
happiness has no bounds.

A soothing, peaceful, deep feeling,
morning is the way of nature's healing.

Music

Music is all around,
All it needs is to feel the sound.

The rustling of leaves in the wind
In the morning, whispers of birds.

In the noise and peace,
In the sky and underneath.

In laughter and cry,
In moments, wet or dry.

Music of happiness in growth,
Music of excitement in speed.

Music resides within you, just feel,
It's a way to forgive and heal.